SURROUNDED BY FRIENDS

BY

SURROUNDED

FRIENDS

MATTHEW
ROHRER

WAVE BOOKS

SEATTLE

NEW YORK

Published by Wave Books

www.wavepoetry.com

Copyright © 2015 by Matthew Rohrer

Wave Books titles are distributed to the trade by

Consortium Book Sales and Distribution

Phone: 800-283-3572 / SAN 631-760X

Library of Congress Cataloging-in-Publication Data

Rohrer, Matthew.

[Poems. Selections]

Surrounded by friends / Matthew Rohrer. — First edition.

pages cm

ISBN 978-1-940696-02-7 (limited edition hardcover) —

ISBN 978-1-940696-03-4 (trade pbk.)

I. Title.

PS3568.O524A6 2015

811'.54—dc23

2014016540

Designed and composed by Quemadura

Printed in the United States of America

9 8 7 6 5 4 3 2 1

First Edition

Wave Books 047

1

2

3

4

To be allowed a friendship with the dead is to be allowed into an infinitely gratifying society, one of which you are a part, one from which no human is excluded, one into which the entirety of what one feels and says is accepted, and accepted whole.

—JOSHUA BECKMAN

FOR MY FRIENDS

1

BICYCLETTE BATAVUS,
FABRIQUÉ EN HOLLANDE, CA. 1904

Do you feel that? he said
how far from home
we are? But the bicycle
didn't answer, it tipped
slightly against the bench.
The forest shadows
came down to the clovers
in the fields. A train
beyond the canal.
He had to admit like the swallows
he was putting off
his long journey back;
100 years ago
in Holland
when they made this bike
their asses were fundamentally different.
And what happens
in all these villages
after we ride through them
on our way back? he said.

But the bicycle didn't answer,
and the two of them
rolled slowly home.
They saw a muskrat in the canal.
Then he tipped his hat to a dog.

SUDDEN SUMMER

Wherever you are in the city
I wish you walked
slightly in front of me
and I could put
my hand on your
shoulder and so relax
you just a little
in the warm wind

we are mayflies
though I look
like a june bug
only here as Cat says
for a short while
like a june bug I fly
into the air

but underground
clacking along
with the R train
slamming me

into the seats
I think of Lucinda
singing *june bug vs. hurricane*
you on my lap
all the windows open
wine-stained teeth

I thought for years
she meant how stirring
and mythic a june bug
battering itself against
a storm but now
I think those were
the names of boxers

and I text you
to see what you think
which is sent
to pending
beneath Cortlandt Street station
which is still imperfect
and will remain
all the days so
though people

come from everywhere to see

water pouring into

the memorial fountain

I'm sure it's beautiful

which is confusing

one woman asked me

how to get to the site

of the terrible disaster

she was holding a map

I said you don't want to

Everything beneath the roof
of trees is sticky
from the trees. Trade éclairs
on a bench because
Does my ass look big?
Everything in the park is reflected
back to beauty. If I find
a moneylender I'm going
to kiss him. The water
comes from lions. It goes
back to water. In a puddle
a sparrow soaks himself
then hops away
to roll in dust. A man
turns and says *Look*
at yourself young man
official society
will never trust you

(he is not speaking to me)

(a little rain blows under the trees)

THERE IS ABSOLUTELY
NOTHING LONELIER

There is absolutely nothing lonelier
than the little Mars rover
never shutting down, digging up
rocks, so far away from Bond Street
in a light rain. I wonder
if he makes little beeps? If so
he is lonelier still. He fires a laser
into the dust. He coughs. A shiny
thing in the sand turns out to be his.

LE MACHINE ATE HIMSELF

Le machine ate himself the card that is mine
I said, and I have need of the card
now, and thank you, I have a grand problem.
She said *le blah blah blah blah blah*
to which I nodded and gave thanks.
Come back in the afternoon, she said
and I said thank you, and I'm dead.

A PAIR OF DUCKS

A pair of ducks and the male
suddenly flies off toward
the boat passing on the river
where I think he might land
then veers off to his purpose
an aerial display with two
farther ducks almost lost
in the rain but I keep
on him I see him
the whole time
while the female
I would say with quiet
exasperation quacks
until he returns to us
quacking drinking beer
on the quai de Bourbon
for minutes at a time
forgetting I am sitting down

BROOKLYN IS COVERED
IN LITTLE PIECES OF PAPER

This is extremely important
what happened to me today
so listen closely
I drew a very appealing
picture of my daughter's
beloved stuffed dog
because she was going
on her first field trip
and was not allowed
to bring the stuffed dog
and I colored in
the picture softly
with a brown pencil
and drew smell lines
coming off his nose
because that is her favorite
aspect of the dog
his smell
so she folded the picture
and put it in her pocket

which is very small
because she is
and we walked to school
through the warm wind
only to find
she had lost the paper
with the picture on it
which was terrible
just terrible
but what could we do?
the green door
was going to open
in two minutes

and on the way home
I thought halfheartedly
I'll look on the ground
for a folded piece
of paper
and when I did
I saw Brooklyn
is covered in little
pieces of paper
which fact I was contemplating

in the bright sun

and the wind pressing papers against

the chain-link fence

when I saw it

my little picture

and bent down

and in my head

a voice said

fuck yeah!

On a pilgrimage to the world's most famous painting
undertaken with blisters I stop instead
at Paolo Caliari, called Veronese, who is very lonely,
his woman with a little doggy has spirit. I think there is
a kind of attention I can pay this painting
that Paolo can feel, though he is dead.
Even his ancient paintings were ruins, and I
too feel like I've been beaten up, all I want is a seat
at the table in the enormous painting called
Le Nozze di Cana which I used to think meant
The Night of the Dog, on account of the dog.

THE PHOTOGRAPHS OF ALLEN GINSBERG
AT THE GREY GALLERY, NYC

Photographs of young people
growing old are like lights on
in a tall building
and the sun still in the sky.
It is a very special melancholy
to be replaced on the streets
surrounded on all sides
by windows
   — a break to text
 are you high?
     — good — the Ginsberg
   photos are great —
   they are much better
 than this poem —
where a traveler takes
a self-portrait
beneath the arch.
And yet there is something
about a photograph
that poisons the heart.

WHERE I LIVED

I live up here,
you live down there,
he said, touching first
my forehead then
my sternum; *come up*
and see me sometime,
and flicked my nose
as he said this,
traveling up from where
I lived to where he lived.
He also said, every time
our family saddled up
to depart, *see you in the*
funny papers, which was
another place he mistakenly
believed I lived, when I lived,
as everyone knew, in an
enormous mitten with a beetle,
a mouse, a hedgehog, a hare,
a badger, and other increasingly

large creatures of the forest,
and waited there for a stranger's
kiss to set me free. His own wife,
my grandmother, knitted it for me.

Eight Romany sisters spread their wings
in the garden. Their gold teeth
are unnerving. Every single
baby is asleep. They want
a little money and I give
them less. I'm charming and
handsome. They take my pen.
I buy the poem from the garden
of bees for one euro. A touch
on the arm. A mystery word.
The sky has two faces.
For reasons unaccountable
my hand trembles.
If the Romany are horrified of bees
they keep it secret.

In the ancient tapestries
were they worse at rendering
reality or worse at rendering
our reality? I ask. The only
answer is the loud dribble
of water running down
the outside of the wall. On my
way home I see the same
Romany girl I bought a poem
from and she recognizes me.
The clouds are whipped up
over the river. In the Palace
of Justice every single one
of those men in their offices
is rich but I feel sorry
for them nonetheless. There is
a kind of poverty to everything.

AUTUMN GLORY

Looking at old pictures
I'm on fire
don't show your dad
how it says *Legalize It*
on the side of the hill
now we are older
it's like that whole place
shifted out from under us
the self is the constant
past which time flies
until a cloud melts
through the wall
it is a translation
of an abstract painting
into a feeling
I don't even have
I have a slight fever
while feeding the kids
and in a dream
they eat candy
on top of me
and when I wake up
autumn glory and candy wrappers

HOW TO LIVE

I wonder if I have any books here
        by Joanne Kyger or are they all
    at work?

That's nice work if you can get it.

I look at my wife on the couch
        she's working.

A cat is sleeping on her
        outside a nor'easter twists up the night.

Hello winter, I say, come on in.
        With huge eyes like an owl
    I open up my heart.

They say that's the only way
        to conquer death, to greet it
    warmly.

All these books!

How to live?

If I tickle my daughter she
stops crying.

Nothing is more important to the ant
whose exoskeleton has been breached
by mushroom spores that are now
controlling his nervous system
and compelling him to climb to a high leaf
only to die and release the spores
over the whole forest
than this poem about his sad plight.

Otherwise his life is meaningless.
Forage. Chew. Recognize by scent.
Abdication of the will. A huge wind
that comes and sweeps his fellows
off the grass. When he dies up there
in the treetops the mushroom grows
right out of his head and breaks open
lightly dusting the afternoon.

Everything he thought he was here
on Earth to do has been left undone.

Through the trees

the spores move on their sinister ways.

I put down the science magazine written

for elementary school kids

in which I have briefly disappeared.

BIRTHDAY SONNET

Morning bombed-out car
smell in the neighborhood
chocolate and almond croissant
when everything else is closed
your new earrings pull down
your ears you are shy like they are
restaurants are too fussy
you just want blue sky
in a little circle overhead
with me it's all the same
overcast days always turn me on
like Paris you are beautiful
though you've been around a while

PAVILION OF LEAVES

Central Park in a
pavilion of leaves
with extra sauce
for midday
is only a snack
and a photograph
of cold cherries
like a young woman's
legs softly peeling
after burning
a pennywhistle
in the distance
with the piping children's
voices which are
distant peace
in a breeze
two white butterflies
trying so hard

The model farm is therapeutic.
The four-horned sheep
has all manner of things
clinging to his wool.
The cow is not angry.
None of the goats are daunted.
My daughter steps into the gravel
near a puddle and leaves a hole
that quickly fills
with water and sees this
and does it again.
On the way out
of one of the buildings
art students have posted
their pencil drawings
of the animals and they
are so accurate
we stop walking.

When I was little
we ate a meal
at my great-grandmother's farm.
She prepared it like she had
for over eighty years. Corn
bread. Bacon. Fried chicken.
Green beans. Lines of black ants
draped over everything, across the food
and led across the table
down the legs
across the floor.
She was what others
would call blind.
But they said stubborn.
My parents made a little sign with their hands
and we sat there
while she ate her ants.

Now that shirt is bittersweet
the president sweeps the globe
there's a chill
after days of terrible heat
whatever you say dear my wife
is washing the dishes
a fantasy baseball game
with my son drags on
to extra innings in Paris
the lights go out
explosion!
the radio DJ gasps and dies
the haunted windows
spread their wings
the stones in the courtyard
go dark in the rain

THERE IS A FLOWER

There is a flower
that only grows
in the forest canopy
someone said its name
I wasn't listening
we only know about it
because it falls
on us as we walk
a faint path
through the pines
and a lower canopy
of nettles
like a burst of dawn
they lie on the path
too fine of strange colors
to belong here
this must be
why the butterflies
spend so much time
up high
get higher

HANK'S SALOON

The first free school in Brooklyn
was here the ecology
of Fulton Mall
is moving slowly
with the music because I am
paying close attention
to the way the city is writing
my poem ordering a large Coke
next to me and a shot
I'm waiting for someone to ask me
where I am which is
pretending to be
a stranger's mother and it costs
money to piss in the city now
it costs money to float like a song

FUCK THE BANKS

you can't even storm out
they have to buzz you out

POEM FOR EDNA ST. VINCENT MILLAY

The next thing I am going to say
is a secret. In World War II
they told Edna St. Vincent Millay
about all the invasions
so she could write a poem
for each one, a poem
like a bottle of champagne
to be smashed against
a ship before it sails
and everyone sat and listened
to the poem
on the radio and imagined
things in his or her mind
that the words weren't really saying
rocking back and forth
in a chair, steam
rising from dinner
she spread all her poems
out across New England
acres of them, dreadful, she said

everyone has her own
version of a lonely life
the temperature drops
20 degrees the kids
are in bed a wind
blows through all the windows
at once knocking the hanging pots
and pans together
like a gentle quake
we hear what we want
to hear the invasion
has been called off
the pots and pans ding
gently in the kitchen
the invasion is what
we want it to be
this is a poem
you can smash against it
before it sails
then finish your dinner
it is not one
of the saddest poems
ever written

Edna St. Vincent Millay
wrote that it's called LAMENT
only one person dies in it
a poem where thousands
of people die
just isn't as sad

2

CROSSING UNDERNEATH
THE WATER

Crossing underneath the water
to Brooklyn it is God
speaking to the young girl
now forced to remove
her headphones. To hear him
speak through the mouth
of a plain overweight
drifter is the miracle.
And she answers him.
She wants to disappear
in something too. She
and he are wearing
the same sneakers.
It's how they met.

MOTHER'S DAY

Mother's Day pollen

and allergies clouds

of allergies flowing

across the park

and baseballs

distant cracks

in the morning

the grass bejeweled

with all the glitz

you didn't buy

your mother

now drinking mimosas

on a blanket

heads up!

some of the children

when they step away

from every pitch

oh it is a shame

and their mothers

step away

BUS PASS

She found a bus pass
on her front steps
with $20 on it
and though she basically
knew it belonged to B.
she just got on the bus.
But wine loosened her
tongue. She cried,
and then she wiped
her eyes and said no,
I won't cry. And indeed
there was no reason.
B. is rich. A fine
sprinkle of ice
fell all across the city.

ANEMOMETER

After the game the coach
punched out the umpire
and the kids piled on
to break his rib
New Jersey strong
the train blew
the dusk past the ball fields

As the sun went on its way
the man lay panting in the dirt
the score was 3–2
they won and then
they punched him out

BULL SHARK

The little girl covers herself with shaving cream
in the bath. The world outside is deeply frozen.
Smoke is the only moving thing.
A little spacey, staring at the tiles. She already
fills the tub when she stretches out.
If a bull shark and a blue shark are coming
toward her, as she says, she's calm.

And now kids!
said the teacher
from the religious school
whose kids were all
over the darkened Hall of the Jellyfish
in the aquarium,
the one thing
about the jellyfish
kids, is that it's
sticky, that's why
it's called a jellyfish
and that's why
it's behind glass.

Wow
said the boys, for they
were all boys
in this religious school.

The only light
in the darkness
was inside the jellyfish.

DARK INSIDE, BRIGHT OUTSIDE, A MAGRITTE

Dark inside, bright outside, a Magritte
painting, white light on magnolia
leaves. A hired gardener working
for the landlord, clearing out
the shadows. The Presidents make
a sound like *rrrrrr* as they pass
each other miles overhead. Right now
on Mars, the lonely rover picks up a strange
shiny object, which has fallen off it.

A PERFUME

The crazy guy

gets back on the train

the sun comes in low

late spring

hundreds of cars and trucks

not going anywhere

on the overpass

near the river

the train enters the earth

the light dims

Crazy has something to say

about salvation

loud and clear

the flowering trees

drop their petals on the land

a perfume blows across the city

SHE STEPPED OUTSIDE

She stepped outside
at dusk wearing
a T-shirt that said
KISS ME I'M LOADED.
The contrails overhead
were pink and at the tip
of one like a spider
spinning it out a very tiny
plane glowed bright pink
in the sunset.
What a beautiful day
she said for the third
or fourth time that day.
It would have felt wrong
not to say so.

DULCIMER AND FLUTE (WHILE SYRIA DESTROYS ITSELF)

There is some kind
of acrid taste
in the wind
that is emotional
and another kind
that smells like
a brewery. A wooden
flute pants somewhere
across the courtyard.
Even with a light rain
the windows open slightly
the chickens in their yard
talking for a while
until the rain is like
a dulcimer on the bricks
and they're quiet. And all
around this tiny planet
enormous chunks of pure
iron are flying in every direction.

Quickly all the little girls
across the country
hurry home in the same
winter coats
a wind winds around
the loud distracted blocks
Friday afternoon lightless
be clear, be clear
a young mother thinks
distracted on Earth
looking always at the clouds
the tin clank
of the outside thermometer
blowing against
the window
is its own forecast

BAD WEATHER PLAN #4

Taped outside the metropolitan
transit authority office
"bad weather plan #4"
and standing beside it
a woman. Everyone who
passes she hands them
a piece of paper.
It's for you
she says.
In all the years
no one has ever
accepted it. Waiting for her bus
a mousy girl complains
about her professor
to someone who is
entirely fictive.

POEM FOR MY SISTER

She was thinking
of a hall carved deep
beneath a mountain
with her eyes closed
when she suddenly
opened them.
She was still on the ferry
but there was a difference
a terrifying music
was coming from the sky.
In this same town
lived a boy and a girl
who could be in different
rooms but know
what the other was drawing.

HE HAS A JOB, BUT IT'S A SAD JOB

He has a job, but it's a sad job.
He has to wear a tie. He drinks
a beer in the church when no one's
looking. Names written in jest
and longing carved in sharp angles
in the bathroom. Night gathers up
the country road. A car he sold
to someone drives away, but the car
is empty. Emptiness is driving the car.

IN THE PARK

Underneath the arch
into the park
he sleeps on a bench
an open umbrella covers
him 19 degrees Fahrenheit blue air
frozen mud
he needs a society that's willing
a few joggers struggle
on the road that crosses
overhead a few strollers
to the library
one of his shoes is
bottomless there is a shopping
cart filled with brickbats
the enormous umbrella
is a private affair
on no ballot is there
the name of someone
who will stop
the police coming
slowly up the path

POEM

The patient steps out
of the doctor's office
into the winter morning.
He has just been told
he has some disease
that doesn't seem
that bad. He is standing
where two subway lines
meet. It doesn't matter
which one he takes.
Both of them take him to work.

SHAMAN FROM THAILAND

A condition of the eye
that makes everything look
like flowers even clouds
the accidental feminine gaze
laughing in the shower
in a photograph
of a shaman
from Thailand
her eyes travel the room
to find you more intense
than any government
and they are not finished
a woman is singing over jazz

AT DANTE'S HOUSE

At Dante's house
there is no poem
until the tour guide
goes silent
on his wireless earphones
and walks away
for just a moment
before the next one comes
I hear the swallows
how quick they are
among their friends
to disappear
behind yellow houses

TWO POEMS FOR ISSA

Role-playing after dinner
to buy a used car
and the role-playing
is rough the car dealer
(who is S.) won't bend
even sitting at the table
with the tortillas I made
I tremble I am not
prepared to spend any money
autumn evening

＊

Autumn evening
the children aren't interested
in the poems of Issa
who died poor hundreds
of years ago
I recycle the children's book
about Issa with a clear mind
it is not Issa himself
who disappears

THE MEDITATIONS OF
MARCUS AURELIUS

Someone plays the piano
from memory it goes on
and on I believe it is from the era
we call Romanticism that is how
I feel about it I also
in the darkened courtyard feel
a storm is coming on
though it's just the afternoon

*

Last day of summer
stripped bare beneath the sun
like a fascist searchlight searching
the park but we're drinking
wine on a blanket underneath
some trees
the kids playing with toy knights
you'll never get me ha
ha ha the knife on the blanket

open so the blade dries
because it's real French steel
with a hint of melon

*

Dazed in the breeze
picnic over S. kisses me I text
her though we're right beside
each other something the kids
don't need to hear
laughter I am happy to discover
in every language is laughter

MAGNOLIA PETALS
FALLING ON BRICKS

Birds freaking out
in the courtyard in song
and smoke from rich
meats. I turn my back
on it to hear it better.
I know the magnolia
has awakened in its
finery and I peek.
Like a beautiful
woman it looks straight
ahead. Like J. said
one time he sat so still
he heard a plant growing;
I hear the petals
on the bricks.
And the little neighbor crying
that her dog got stitches.

HELLO MERMEN

A brief note left
in the hold of a ship
hello mermen
do us a favor
and turn the record
over we never want
the past to disappear
when I found it
and read it aloud
at the bar everyone
laughed it seemed
too sad

HOMAGE TO
ATTILA JÓZSEF

I don't think
we should be citizens
of anything but ideas
oh József they let you
out of jail but the stars
were your jailers
here I am in Europe
soaking wet and
a little sad

VOLKSWAGEN RABBIT

Kelly you were so tall!
You had long legs
and you did a good job
shaving them. Something
incredibly complicated was going on
in America 1987.
I drove you to your car.
Your curly hair in the late
afternoon on the prairie.
And then you went
to Belgium and died.

POEM FOR VIRGIL BĂNESCU

Bear and reindeer cut up on a plate.
An endless cave.
A duvet of darkness.
Your notes piping and plaintive I think
are still down there though
they traveled ahead of you
too. They walked all the way
back to the vineyards
where we slept. You were
now and then just a tiny
bit cruel to children
because you were a child.

3

POEM WRITTEN WITH BUSON

In a minute
among the river reeds
I will debut my composition
a urine-stained quilt
is the flag of
early summer rain
and when I open my mouth
not even a bird singing
contains all my ideas
for rising and falling all day
my phone vibrates
its tiny mouth
in the mountain's shadow

POEM WRITTEN WITH BASHŌ

After drinking last night
I climbed into the air
and slept badly, a stiff neck
a bridge of flowers
led me into the morning
high above the skylarks.
The children ate cereal
under a gloomy sky, and sadly,
the girl loves her mother
more than she loves me.
I drink from a downpour
and choose her socks
with tiny whales.
I wrote her a song
about our pressing need
to grocery-shop
until it was clear, the mirror
showed a few more years
and a disappointing doughnut.
Let that be my name.

POEM WRITTEN WITH BASHŌ

As fog clears away
from the sad lake
in the park
I cling like ivy
to my wife at night
midway across a bridge
in a complicated dream
of a hotel on the moon
I wake up with only broken bones
I don't have the courage
to blink
it is Thursday
just like that
a great wind
boils the harbor
as though looking for someone

POEM WRITTEN WITH BUSON

The whole country
in a courtly dance
its tiny mouth open
I pour another cup of wine
and falling, rising
the children remove their toys
around the small apartment
to their bunk beds
not quite dark yet
early spring with snow
on the wind
the woman across the street
bent like a sickle
collecting bottles and cans
knocks, goes on
I wonder where she lives
and the stars shining
on her greasy clothes

POEM WRITTEN WITH BASHŌ

I began to doubt myself
borrowed a woman's nightgown
and walked through the park
to see poems pasted to a wall.
I took such a deep breath
the tide rose almost to my door.
Friends too far away
while dawn arrives
I send them a text
and sleep awhile.
I know a little light goes on
in the sound of wind.

POEM WRITTEN WITH ISSA

A friend emails

how much are you

enjoying yourself?

a dripping faucet

loose cat litter

no doubt about it

a good world

is difficult I say

as if I were

tilling a field

ashamed of myself

I apologize

to the sleeping child

POEM WRITTEN WITH ISSA

Working in the sun

from now on

I vow to smile

to me, to the mountain

and mean it

as soon

as the snow goes

as soon

as the children apologize

to each others' coats

and turn out their light

the moon and the flowers

are quietly speaking

to each other

spring rain

so cold it crackles

POEM WRITTEN WITH ISSA

Spring break
in a dim room
with a glass of wine
is what it is.
A drunk wrecked
my truck.
The moon and flowers
against me.
In the most
favorable light
today is pale gray.
Hey sparrow!
I have another hour
under all these flowers.

POEM WRITTEN WITH ISSA

In my dream

his voice began to fade

I had to call him

the next day

I feel about average

he said

I'm going out

to buy some juice

a huge frog

was in the driveway

a small boat drifting

the river flowed in silence

POEM WRITTEN WITH BASHŌ

A photograph
on the back of a hand mirror
resembles someone you knew
who sang themselves utterly away.
It cannot touch you
or the sound of the rapids.
Leave it, and walk farther
crawling up my leg
to find me all smiles
attached to nothing.
You and I can stay
in the morning dew.
My little telephone
in the mulberry fields
going unanswered
on that blade of grass.

POEM WRITTEN WITH BUSON

This new weather isn't good for me
mixed with small shells
but somehow the chrysanthemum
has a personality
and sleeps with me awhile.
What is true today
pricked by the cold's needle
beside the sea
is this bucket of azaleas.
My wife with our kids
through the dunes
as the sound fades
into a single-engine plane.

POEM WRITTEN WITH BASHŌ

The sound of the water jar
empties in the open graves
where the refugees live.
Because it does not touch me
near my pillow
I can sleep and dream
of the clean lines
of summer. What I thought
were faces turn out
to be elaborate plates of sweets
not this human sadness.
One or two inches above
my head until the mosquito
sticks his snout
into my dream.

POEM WRITTEN WITH ISSA

Phone on my stomach
waiting to see
whether she texts me back
the night shifts
across the earth
like a blanket
that's too small
under the summer rain
the skinny cat leaps up
the moon on her hands

POEM WRITTEN WITH BASHŌ

Cat drinking from the running faucet
the moon his only companion
the past isn't as far away as we think
even vines cling for their lives
I empty a bottle of wine
in a stiff spring breeze
old friends come back to say
wake up! wake up!

1

Might as well spend money
on wine instead of new clothes

Might as well pour all the wine on these books

Might as well get drunk in a bar

Might as well pour myself
a tearful glass of fire

Might as well stop dreaming
of heaven, legless

Might as well unlearn
the smell of your hair

I am old

2

I poured out my heart
to her in a letter
I said it was the end of the world

I said my face is wet with tears
and that's my best feature

What a waste of time
How many of the ancients' love poems
actually worked?

The doctor said she was ill

The wind blew the clouds
away from the moon

The next day was beautiful

I knew it would be embarrassing
to be seen walking around
outside her apartment

I went to the bar

3

I moved to the city
I was going to be great
Now I have to leave

I can't afford to eat properly
the way you eat

The pigeons cooing in the evening
used to lull me to sleep

"O heart be joyful" I read
on a restroom wall

It was a terrible lie

Misfortune rises all the way
to heaven

But this too shall pass

4

I said it before
and I'll say it again
it's not my fault

Like a parrot I said
what everyone else said

Roses and weeds
are exactly the same

I'm still looking for someone
who thinks I'm cool

With wine stains all over my shirts
I'm not trying to hide anything

Sometimes I dream
I'm happy

　　　　Drinking wine
　　　　makes me happy

5

It's pouring rain out
Let's get a drink

It's too muddy
to take a walk
Let's get a drink

Or you could bring some wine over
and some flowers

Because the bars are closed
even if you bang on the doors

The rain is beautiful
for about five minutes
and then it's annoying

your red lips
making a circle
replace the sun

If I'm lucky

6

May you never have to sit
in a doctor's waiting room

May everything blow over

You are too beautiful
for that

The autumn winds rip off
the leaves
but the tree remains

May you move unmolested
through the city

And if anyone even looks
at you wrong
may they burn in hell

Just leave it to me

7

All I want to do
is get drunk with my wife

An endless glass of wine
both of us on the floor

So what if squares
look down on us?

Boring and misguided
are their miserable lives

When my wife is in the city
and I'm home
I want to cry

The moonlight
on the cypress tree
is a bitter light

No book has ever kissed me
like she does

8

The city is a beautiful place

The summer night lingers
just above the streets

And there is something
that frightens off the timid

Those who are drawn here
have a duty to prolong it

And gladly will they

Every evening in the city
is a deep pool of wine

Everyone who lives in the city
is drunk with it

And cannot leave

They are surrounded by friends

9

In the morning
when I went into my garden
to pick a rose
a nightingale started to freak out

which
the more I thought about it
freaked me out

There was a deep and terrible connection

I could not bear

In a garden we believe
life is eternal

Which we don't even want

The brisk wind pouring down
from the north
reminds me of my friend

It has the same cold magnificence

I lean out the window
and call out a sort of greeting

I know he is happy
he is doing well

I have followed him
many times
into the unlikeliest bars

Even hecklers
cannot spoil his fun

THE EMPEROR

She sends me a text
she's coming home
the train emerges
from underground

I light the fire under
the pot, I pour her
a glass of wine
I fold a napkin under
a little fork

the wind blows the rain
into the windows
the emperor himself
is not this happy

ACKNOWLEDGMENTS

Some of these poems have already appeared in the following
journals:

The Academy of American Poets POEM-A-DAY

The American Poetry Review

The American Reader

Barrelhouse

Coldfront

El Aleph Anthology

Ep;phany

Harper's

Le Zaporogue (Denmark)

Logue (Norway)

The New York Times Magazine

Poetry

The Rumpus

TRANSLATIONS FROM HAFIZ also appeared as a limited edition
chapbook, published by Wave Books on the occasion of *Three
Days of Poetry: Poetry in Translation* at the Henry Art Gallery in
Seattle, 2011.

95

THE EMPEROR first appeared as a part of the Academy of American Poets POEM-A-DAY project, and then in *She Walks in Beauty: A Woman's Journey Through Poems*, edited by Caroline Kennedy, Hyperion, 2011.

I would like to thank the editors and volunteers who helped make all of these.

Special thanks to Joshua Beckman, Matthew Zapruder, Anthony McCann, Noelle Kocot, and Susan McCullough for their careful attention and advice. Thank you, Jeff, again.

I would like to especially thank Robert Hass, for his beautiful book *The Essential Haiku*, and for his permission to borrow some of it.

Thank you, friends